*The desert . . . . its sky, its air, its flaming sunsets and dramatic landscapes . . . . all this, yet a strange, mysterious more. And it is of this that the Meadowlark sings. Under his spell the load is always lighter . . . .*

# Birds

## OF THE SOUTHWESTERN

# Desert

*Gusse Thomas Smith*

*Illustrated by Harriet Morton Holmes*

*Published by*
GEM GUIDES BOOK COMPANY
*315 Cloverleaf Drive, Suite F*
*Baldwin Park, California 91706*

# Cast of Characters . . .

ll birds are happy and freely tell you so. They're the best of friends to cultivate and, with birds, that's fairly easy to do.

Over four hundred kinds of birds find their favorite altitude, climate and essential food in the lower Sonoran life-zone, which is the desert country below three thousand feet. Much of the bird population lives here permanently — either stays for the winter or the summer or drops in casually for visits. You'll find them everywhere in desert country — living, loving, singing, luring you to follow them.

The most frequently seen of the desert birds are introduced informally in this book. With a minimum of effort you can see them all and know them by name in a few weeks. Some will strongly resemble their eastern cousins, some differ to an interesting degree, while others must be seen here or not at all.

With best wishes, I give you my birds.

*Grace Thomas Smith.*

*SAGUAROLAND*

# BIRDS OF THE SAGUARO

•

THE oldest continuously operated apartment house in the world is the Saguaro, or Giant Cactus. It towers above all other desert growth and no matter how little it may resemble one, it is a tree.

In a Department of Interior book entitled "Birds of the Saguaro National Monument", H. S. Swarth states there are five kinds of birds entirely dependent upon its presence and that "it is useless to look for them where this cactus does not grow". They are the Mearn's Gilded Flicker, the Gila (hela) Woodpecker, the Arizona Crested Flycatcher, the Saguaro or Mexican Screech Owl, and, most interesting of all, the tiny Elf Owl. Other birds which freely nest in or on the Saguaro but which occur elsewhere are the Western Red-tailed Hawk, Swainson Hawk, American Sparrow Hawk, Western Horned Owl, Ash-throated Flycatcher, Purple Martin, House Finch, and occasionally the Mourning Dove.

With such an assortment of tenants no manager less inspired than Dame Nature herself could stay in business a week, yet she has kept a workable peace on the premises for centuries. However, taking life in the Saguaro Apartments the year round, many are its comedies and tragedies. The struggle there for existence is as intense and engrossing and the individualities of its residents as pronounced and divergent as any found in the great world. From dawn to dusk nest digging, 'chiseling', feeding, scolding, neighborly spying, and family gossip all go on; each according to his own nature. From dusk to dawn quick Owls dart in and out like ghosts with dainty morsels for their babies, never rousing the house.

Saguaroland is a tiny, separate world. No observer can see it all, but once glimpsed it stirs the imagination forever.

*Upper left: Gila Woodpecker*
*Upper right:*
*Arizona Crested Flycatcher*
*Lower: Mearn's Gilded Flicker*

8

# Mearn's Gilded Flicker

(Colaptes chrysoides mearnsi)

*Average length 13 inches*

THIS handsome, *oversized Woodpecker* is a rakish fellow with a *red "mustache" against a gray throat above a yellowish, black-dotted vest.* Under his wings and tail he is strikingly yellow but his upper coloring is mostly a light, clean brown with black bars on his wings.

Anyone in the least acquainted with *Flickers* would recognize him easily from his family mannerisms of flight and voice but his activities in the west are strikingly different from those of the eastern branch. He doesn't run up a smooth surface and pick out a favorable spot to dig; in the desert he must deal with an accordion-pleated tree trunk with clusters of inch long spines running in rigid rows the entire length.

I watched him solve his problem this way. From the top of a tall saguaro he surveyed all the others in the neighborhood, decided upon a home site and flew directly to a spot on a nearby cactus. With no diddling about, he tangled his specialized claws in two clusters of spines on a vertical ridge, sitting slightly sidewise with his bristle-tipped tail feathers braced in the spines of the parallel ridge behind him. He immediately began to peck a circle about three and a half inches in diameter across the ridge in front, into the next valley, and back to his starting place. It looked easy. His bill is sharp as an ice pick, his neck long, his head slender and, like the heads of all *Woodpeckers*, constructed to compensate shock violent enough to cause concussion in other birds. So the actual digging was easy because the pulp of the saguaro, though firm, is not hard like wood. His head bounced like a trip hammer until his doorway was definitely outlined, then he flew away.

I did not see that nest completed but, no doubt, it was excavated horizontally for a few inches then dug straight down ten, twelve, perhaps fifteen inches, roughly in the shape of a half-gallon fruit jar. From the first to the last peck the saguaro cooperated, exuding a viscous sealing juice to harden into solid wood and make the nest more lasting than the cactus itself. In this way the saguaro also protects itself. No matter how many holes are drilled into its body it suffers no injury whatever.

The *Mearn's Gilded Flicker* and the *Gila Woodpecker* dig all the hundreds of holes you see in the saguaro but, by a gentleman's agreement, manage not to interfere with one another. The *Gila Woodpecker* likes altitude so he never works below fourteen feet above ground. The *Flicker* prefers to live on the lower floors so he never digs above the fourteen foot line.

# Gila Woodpecker

(CENTURUS UROPYGIALIS)

*Average length 9 inches*

THIS *Woodpecker* and the *Gilded Flicker* work alike and accomplish almost identical results but there is no reason to confuse the two. The *Gila Woodpecker* is smaller and less dressy. *His head and underparts are a uniform, grayish brown, his wings and tail barred, zebra fashion, with black and white. His only decoration is a bright red cap on his crown.* Also, in contrast to the mild mannered *Flicker*, he lives with a perpetual chip on his shoulder and is peevish with his neighbors.

The family life of both species is full of drudgery and disappointment. Often, after days of digging, before they can occupy their new holes themselves, other birds crowd in and set up housekeeping; in which case, strange to say, both accept their hard luck with little complaint, and altruistically start other holes nearby. Both male and female dump twigs and dead grass into the cavity before any eggs are laid, then the mother bird sits in the dark. When the babies come both parents face the age-old yet modern problem of catering to children impossible to satisfy. However, the least of their worries seems to be finding water — the juicy saguaro pulp takes care of that. Insects form a major part of all food consumed but any juicy fruit or pulp is proudly carried home.

The young are thoroughly spoiled brats when they leave the nest. They refuse to feed themselves just as long as possible and follow their parents around squabbling for tidbits until they are almost full grown.

When the saguaro fruit is ripe in July and August the family feasts en masse with all the diverse colony living in this beneficent cactus. They bury their faces in the luscious red pulp, hunting out every black seed, and life then is at its best. In time of storm they dodge back into their holes and peek out with ludicrous complacence. No nest built in the open could be so cool in summer, so warm in winter, nor so snug and safe from all attack.

# *Arizona Crested Flycatcher*

(MYIARCHUS TYRANNULUS MAGISTER)

*Average length 10 inches*

ALTHOUGH the *Arizona Crested Flycatcher* has a high, stiff crest he is not a notably handsome bird. *His back is grayish olive, his head and wings are all dark brown, and his underparts a sulphur yellow.* He so closely resembles his relative, the smaller *Ash-throated Flycatcher*, there is little point in trying to be sure which is which; the latter showing only a less pronounced coloration and no real crest, only a high pompadour. However, in parts of the desert where the saguaro does not grow there need be no doubt. *The Crested Flycatcher will not be there* — he sticks to the giant cactus belt.

Here he appears in early summer and selects for himself a ready-made saguaro hole fifteen or twenty feet above ground, which automatically means the old nest of a *Gila Woodpecker*. Thereafter he is not fastidious. On top of all debris left by former occupants male and female simply crowd in snake skins, chunks of hair from dead animals and any miscellaneous trash easily picked up on the desert. Egg laying occurs in early June and a noisy, noisome summer follows.

Their diet includes not only all available insects but many small lizards and baby animals of various kinds. Of all the birds on the desert these *Flycatchers* pay least attention to water, in fact they seem to disdain it even when it is in reach.

They are very pugnacious when their personal whims are disregarded. For this reason all the other birds of the saguaro ignore them and allow them to live what seems to be an isolated life in a crowded community.

*Flycatchers* are exceptionally valuable as insect destroyers. They interest me—all birds do—but beyond that, they fail to arouse any yearning to know them more intimately. Their housekeeping is too offensive and their manners too devoid of charm.

# Elf Owl

(MICROPALLAS WHITNEYI)

*Average length 5 inches*

THIS tiniest of all *Owls* is found nowhere else on earth except where the saguaros grow. The best way to see him is to camp overnight in a saguaro 'forest', keep a low fire flickering, and sit very still. He will come to catch bugs in the light. Look quickly—he moves fast, on wings with softened margins that make no swish at all. Like a sparrow-sized ghost he swoops and is gone, but comes again and again. You'll see he is *grayish brown with pale rust mottlings; his wings spotted white*. He'll wear a white muffler under his chin and have cute little white eyebrows in his round, hook-nosed face giving him an ever-startled look.

His claws are weak and small and he loves a good joke better than a fight.

If you manage to catch him he'll play dead and hold the pose just as long as it takes to fool you, but the instant your hand relaxes he'll dart away into the night and have a good hoot beyond your reach.

His most comical trick comes when he is cornered and cannot fly. It would do no good to play dead, so he plays he's not a bird at all by spreading one wing forward in an abnormal position and distorting his whole body like a contortionist, all the while peeking through his feathers with round, yellow eyes.

A show like that is worth the price to anybody.

# Mexican Screech Owl

(OTUS ASIO CINERACEUS)

*Average length 7 inches*

ANOTHER little *Owl*, only an inch or two larger than the *Elf Owl*, the *Mexican Screech Owl*, always lives in the saguaro if he is in the desert, but he is not so dependent as to be found nowhere else.

He is *ashy gray, has feathered toes, conspicuous ear tufts, and a ridiculous monkey face.*

The first one of these I ever saw was on a street car. He sat, supercilious and undisturbed, on the finger of a little boy who held his thumb pressed over the little *Owl's* strong, gripping claws. He probably did not know his garrulous habits around home and his inordinate curiosity in regard to outsiders had been his undoing. The last I saw of him he was glaring at the motorman with every appearance of refusing to pay his fare.

# Western Meadowlark

(STURNELLA NEGLECTA)

*Average length mature, second year, 11 inches*

MY oldest friend is the *Meadowlark*. When I came into Arizona by the back door, lived alone in a desert shack, and prayed the Sun to make my baby well, this strange land of creosote and cactus terrified me. But that very first day the *Meadowlarks* sang, and all the flat miles to the horizon changed before my eyes—and became my home forever.

Always the sudden song of a *Meadowlark* transforms my world like a vision. From a worrying clod, my spirit becomes a dancer above the clouds. A little Chinese girl in a

Christian school, writing a sample of free verse, expressed the Meadowlark's idea exactly:

> *God is my father .... the earth is my mother*
> *Heaven is my home .... why bother?*

The desert banishes bother; its sky, its air, its flaming sunsets and dramatic landscapes; all this—but a strange, mysterious more—and it is of this the *Meadowlark* sings; the spirit of the desert, the triumph of courage, the freedom of strength. Under his spell the load is always lighter.

The *Western Meadowlark* is much larger than his eastern cousin and has more notes of pure tone and greater splendor. He sings on open ground or atop fence posts, and is the easiest of all desert birds to see because of his *bright yellow vest and conspicuous black necktie.* He wears a *grayish brown, black-and-white-barred coat with white edge trim and has a proud up-standing carriage.* He loves roadsides, ranches, resort hotels, Mexican villages, canal banks, city parks, Indian reservations, golf courses—why bother, a good mixer is happy anywhere.

Both male and female cooperate in building the nest, usually on the ground in heavy grass or thorny thickets— the grass or brush pulled over, dome fashion, for protection. This makes it hard for us to find, but leaves it tragically easy for the snakes and the coyotes during the thirteen days of incubation and the twelve days afterward that the babies stay in the nest.

Open country and accessible water seem to be the *Meadowlark's* first requirements but a seventy per cent insect and thirty per cent vegetable food supply must be in reasonable reach. They nest very early in the spring which comes to the desert sometimes in February. It is then he sings with greatest enthusiasm though he sings all winter, in fact all year, even in December occasionally.

# Cactus Wren

(Heleodytes brunneicapillus)

*Average length 8½ inches*

THE *Cactus Wren* has been designated by the Árizona Legislature as the state bird. It was the highest tribute that august body could pay but, even so, it is not this bird's greatest distinction. Long before man formed legislatures she had subdued to her own use the devil of the desert, the deadly cholla cactus. It takes character to do that. Besides, something about this largest form of the two hundred and fifty North American *Wrens* impels, in generalization, the use of the feminine pronoun, instead of the usual 'he'. It takes personality to do that.

And she isn't even beautiful—just *all over brownish*

*with dashes of white above, and coalescing brown spots on the lighter underside; with heavy, rounded tail spotted white along the outer edges*—as birds go, she isn't even pretty. But she is fearless and determined; an ingenious homemaker, a cheerful and wise mother. Almost too independent in a self-satisfied sort of way.

I sat on a warm rock one coolish March day and spied into her home life in its serenest phase. Her bright, alert eyes peered out at me from deep in her elongated, almost horizontal nest inserted like an oversized milk bottle in millions of fiendish spines of a large cholla cactus. Such a nest could only have been constructed from the outer edge inward. Carrying a streamer of dried grass she had first alighted at a natural opening in the cholla branches, and had woven, with the most delicate precision, a threshold there, anchored in the naked, ivory-hard spines themselves. After this she had worked forward into the heart of the plant, twig by twig, one grass fiber at a time, until her structure was roughly outlined. An incredible achievement—if you know chollas!

The main chamber was larger than the entrance, in milk bottle proportions, and the whole about twelve inches from the back wall to the door. In the early stages needles stuck through the interlaced twigs and lined her walls with death. To cover these she must fetch enough soft material to thickly pad at least the floor where her babies must live. A surprising quantity of feathers, leaves, hairs, and the down of innumerable desert plants are required to carpet even so small an area; a long and exacting task since after each tiny load she must tread the whole surface into the firmness of felt.

Brooding there that day, with her eggs warm against her breast, my little *Wren* felt safe from all things—and, heaven knows, she was from me, and from the hawk, the snake, the rat, the fox, even the slinking coyote but, poor dear, there would come a day when her fledglings must take the air. Among brush and tree-dwelling birds the youngsters often muff test flights, grounding directly beneath the starting point. So I gazed in shuddering apprehension at the ground around the base of the cholla, covered widely with waiting segments from the parent devil, black now but full of spines more treacherous than those above. But the business of life must go on and I knew the babies would make a try. Some, perhaps, would escape. The desert is a stern home, exacting courage and strength from all its children.

But don't feel too sorry for the desert birds. They live there from preference and, comparatively, only a few *Wrens* stray across to the cultivated acres. It is always in the open desert their astonishing nests catch the eye. They build nests in season and out of season, seemingly for the love of it, and only the brooding nest is bottle-shaped and covered over. The cock, who has been left out of this account so far, builds nest after nest all for himself in the tops of the cholla, wide open to the sun—to establish his presence, perhaps, although he rests in them at times, or does a little off key singing, which would bring shame to his eastern cousins.

*Cholla Cactus . . .*
*most fiendish of*
*them all*

# Inca Dove

(Scardafella Inca)

*Average length 8 inches*

**D**OVES are everywhere—in the streets, along the canals, on the lawns, in the fields, and far out into the chaparral. They are so numerous and so trusting they are practically underfoot the year round anywhere in the Valley of the Sun.

This is particularly true of the dainty *Inca Dove* who walks abroad like a mincing little lady. She has such a cajoling, gentle voice some call her the "wooing" bird though she is such a quick fighter among her own kind I fear she likes the wooing better than the wedding. Why not? She knows she is beautiful with her *pink breast, carmine legs, and long, graceful tail of brownish gray, edged with clean white. Her top coat is the most delicate of all the dove grays.* She nests in garden shrubs or low trees anywhere, and lies on flat limbs to give such insistent love calls she means to me the dreamy illusion of the desert itself.

*Mexican Ground Doves,* often seen in the same localities, are easily distinguished from the *Inca* because of their short, spindling tails. They often chatter together in low, pleasant excitement and feed in mixed flocks. So, watch their tails if you would know them apart.

# Western Mourning Dove

(Zenaidura Macroura Marginella)

*Average length 12 inches*

**T**HE large *Western Mourning Dove* is remarkable for the irridescent quality of its plumage. His *body is a rich golden brown, shading to pinkish fawn, color below, with iridescent black spots on back and wings and the sides of his head. His neck and head show a bluish rinse and positively*

*Upper: Western White-winged Dove*
*Center: Western Mourning Dove*
*Lower: Inca Dove*

*glitter with iridescence. His long, slender tail is pointed and bordered with black and white.*

The *Mourning Dove* puffs out his throat and spreads himself tremendously when making love, but nest building seems to take all self-assurance out of the cockiest male. I've watched him puttering for hours carrying twigs and grass to some impossible place where his lady waited. Neither one of them ever seemed to have the least idea of how to use the material effectively. They'll work on a narrow window ledge for days, persistently knocking off most of their accumulation, but showing no signs of discouragement. If he wants to rest she'll actually push him off the ledge and force him to keep up his efforts. No matter where they finally build they never succeed in fashioning a neat, sturdy nest, and after the eggs are laid they'll desert them at the slightest alarm. But somehow there are always large numbers of *Mourning Doves* in the air, or perched on wires, or fences, or in trees, where they coo-coo with a vehemence annoying to some visitors who think they say 'too-late, too-late, too-late'.

# Western White-winged Dove

(MELOPELIA ASIATICA MEARNSI)

*Average length 11 inches*

THE *White-winged Dove* is quite pigeon-like in appearance and actions. He seems grayer than the other doves *and in flight shows a white band across his squarish tail, and glaring, crescent-shaped white patches on his wings.* He is a summer resident, arriving late in April in thousands. His favorite nesting place is in the outlying mesquite and his building ability is much like that of the *Mourning Dove*.

All *Doves* are seed eaters and over the grain fields they may be seen in clouds at any time during the summer. At dusk they regularly fly to water and it is then the hunters lie in wait during the open season. The *White-wings*, in particular, range far out over the desert, especially when the saguaro is ripe. During that season they appear to use lipstick from dipping so deeply into the red saguaro pears.

The voice of the *White-wing* is not soothing and ingratiating like dove tones usually are. It is rather taunting and impudent and in no danger of being mistaken for those of the *Inca* or the *Mourning Dove.*

# Curve-billed Thrasher

(TOXOSTOMA CURVIROSTRE)

*Average length 11½ inches*

TOWNS do not interest the *Curve-billed Thrasher*— even ranches hold little attraction, but in the open desert he is abundant. Swarth says "Arizona is apparently the headquarters of the thrasher family, for whereas in most parts of the United States there is but a single species in any one region, the Arizona valleys contain six of more or less common occurrence."

*Curve-billed Thrashers* are the largest and predominate in number and distribution; easy to find in one sense of the word, but exasperating to observe. You lose him right under your eyes since he is plain desert 'dobe color with no noticeable markings. Look quickly enough and you see he has *a long curved bill, a long, slender tail, and a brownish body, as long but more streamlined than the robin's.* They are shy birds, too, which doesn't help any; stay on the ground, disappearing with amazing speed into the chaparral.

But they are glorious singers, beyond comparison; and they are ardent, spectacular lovers. By slipping along quietly, then standing still for a very long time, I witnessed one love scene near my desert shack. Three *Thrashers* came circling close to the ground; one dignified, two flouncing like overheated popcorn. The aloof one was the debutante being wooed. She posed graciously on a slight eminence of open ground to watch her lovers compete—which they certainly did, singing spasmodically, while bumping and shoving each other for the center of the stage. At times both were in the air, legs dangling, wings flashing, soaring then tumbling drunkenly to dance and ruffle on the ground with quivering bodies, their high-stepping feet inventing fancy steps—all with desperate fervor. When the end came it brought no touching fade-out. Suddenly the lady made up her mind— with a vengeance. Too quickly to see how it happened she joined her favorite and the two of them attacked the jilted one with beak and claw. Instantly all three changed character. The 'broken hearted' flew jauntily to the north practicing a new song to use next time; the aloof lady became over-indulgent; and the eternal male cockily shook his feathers, said 'come along—you' and flew to the south without once looking back to see if his bride were following.

He knew she would.

And she did.

# Gambel Quail

(Lophortyx gambelii)

*Average length 10 inches*

THE most beautiful ground bird you'll ever see is the stately *Gambel Quail*, able to run with speed yet maintain his dignity. You can see him almost anywhere—in pairs —in small groups—in coveys running into the hundreds, very frequently from your car as you drive along outlying country roads.

He always looks dressed up and on his way to a party, *his rufous head adorned with a tall, club-shaped black plume, slightly decurved. His face is a gleaming black, set apart from his black throat by a sharp U-shaped white line. His back is bluish gray with wing edges showing narrow white lines; breast, clear gray, touched far down with a black patch edged with buff.* This gentleman loves color and wears it with taste and distinction while his fat little lady does her best to imitate him in a modest way.

They range far and wide until nesting season, which occurs in late March and April and continues most of the summer. Then water becomes an important factor. The nest must be located near enough to a constant supply for newly hatched babies to walk to it the first day; otherwise they perish, unless excessive dews save them until they are stronger.

The nest is only a shallow depression, scratched in the ground under suitable cover, and lined with dry grass, but it must be big enough to hold ten or twelve buff, brown-spotted eggs. It is fortunate the number is so large as depredations by snakes and coyotes are. distressingly frequent in addition to havoc wrought by occasional desert rain storms. But in spite of all these dangers and the strange habits of men with guns, thousands of beautiful *Gambel Quail* dart about on the desert the year round and add interest to the landscape.

# Pyrrhuloxia

(Pyrrhuloxia sinuata)

*Average length 9 inches*

THE *Pyrrhuloxia* is long on looks but short on music. He is the gray grosbeak, cardinal-like in actions, sometimes seen on the ground but mostly aloft in thorny tangles. He loves ironwood trees. Here he perches on the higher branches where he sits in silence in the early morning or late afternoon. From below, he shows more *deep rose* than *gray* although books describe *him as mainly gray; which, of course, refers to his upper parts. Looking up, you see his yellow parrot bill; his stately crest, face, throat, breast, and underparts of his wings all a lovely clear rose red (on the pink side). The folded wings and the tail are rather a dullish pink.* He looks more like a picture than a bird as I watch him; that gay, bird quality seems lacking. Perhaps he's grieving because he cannot sing, but if he had a mirror to see how magnificent he looks surely he'd defy nature and sing anyway. Birds are so out of our reach. We cannot really know them. The walls of their world are invisible but we can never pass through; only stand outside, look and wonder why this beauty is never gay.

*Pyrrhuloxias* nest early among the thorns, building neatly of twigs, coarse grass, with fine fibers for lining. If you approach too near they voice a worried little purring 'cheek-cheek' full of plaintive friendliness. No one can hear that sound and remain unmoved.

# Roadrunner or Chaparral Cock

### (Geococcyx californianus)

*Average length 24 inches*

NOW there's a bird for you—the desert clown, unique to this region and like nothing you ever saw on land or sea. The *Roadrunner* is a ground dweller of the cuckoo family, two feet long, with a bill longer than his head and an appetite longer than his tail. His wings are stubby and ineffective for distance flying, his plumage always looks shabby, and raising or lowering his bristle-tipped top-knot, he always looks absurdly surprised. Around his mocking eyes he has a naked yellow ring seemingly emphasized with mascara on his stiff eyelashes—yes, eyelashes. He is *streaked with brown and white, glossed with steel blue, changing toward the tail to bronzy green. His long tail feathers are blue-black and green, tipped with white. His throat and underparts are a dirty white, dashed with black.* You'd think with all that to work with he could look quite dressy, but he never does. A bedouin, a true son of the desert—but never a vagabond.

At first sight he appears tail heavy—but his best stunts depend on that tail. He is a speed demon and will race anything from a horned toad to a Cadillac; and when he is quite sure he has won, he will turn off to the side, throw his tail in the air, dig his toes in the ground, and look back in impudent astonishment. Though wild and lawless he makes an amusing pet, not at all shy, ready to eat anything he can swallow, and an inveterate show-off—quite a ventriloquist at times. Ranchers like him around the barnyard and all Mexicans love him as their loyal "Paisano".

The nesting habits of *Roadrunners* are about as irregular and unusual as their other traits. Really tame ones will invade a desert shack and try to settle behind the woodbox; or,

ROADRUNNER or CHAPARRAL COCK

in the barn; though under usual conditions they'll throw together an immense mass of sticks and trash on the ground under low brush, or in the lower branches of mesquite or palo verde trees. They trample this down in the middle after a fashion, and line the depression with snake skins, feathers, any soft things they can steal off nearby clotheslines. At irregular intervals from three to nine elliptical white eggs appear in the midst of this confusion. They are so erratic about laying eggs and the temperature of the desert is so warm that babies of various ages get mixed up with perfectly fresh eggs and mother's work is never done.

*Roadrunners* are courageous and self-supporting and do an enormous amount of good in the world. They eat incredible numbers of the very pests man wants most to be rid of —grasshoppers, crickets, caterpillars, beetles, centipedes, mice, lizards and, most important of all, snakes—lots of snakes.

It is a thrilling, three hour show to see a *Roadrunner* kill a big rattler, literally worrying it to death, leaping and dive bombing to deliver stab after stab at the base of the brain. If the victim is not too large, not much longer than the bird, it is another three hour show to watch him swallow it head first. It is a desperate business and a lot of snake is visible a long time—I could never quite stay to the end.

*Roadrunners* live the year round in a chosen locality, developing a regular schedule in covering their beat. One passed in front of my desert cottage at the same time midmorning every day for several months; and I, as regularly, watched for him. He was always in a terrific hurry and intensely concentrated on finding food—lots of food. He and his whole family were ridden by slave driving appetites and the more I watched him fighting to live, the better I realized that if he occasionally stopped at a Meadowlark's nest, he was forced by necessity rather than innate meanness.

*30*

# Black Phoebe

(SAYORNIS NIGRICANS)

*Average length 6 inches*

THE swirling, swooping *Black Phoebe* loves waterways and builds queer wall-pocket nests of mud pellets mixed with dry grass and bark strips under bridges or on nearby walls and cliffs. These birds are easy to identify, and not at all difficult to locate as they live in swarming groups and constantly call to one another in sweet, plaintive tones.

Perched or flying they appear *black with abruptly white underside, the little black head* so prominently domed it seems almost crested. Inordinately busy about their own affairs they pay no attention to cars passing a bridge they live under or to observers who pause to watch their activities.

They fly forty or fifty feet in the air, dive straight down towards the water, almost skim its surface, then sail in eccentric arcs, snapping insects on the wing. From morning to night the show is unforgettable—the actors so lively and so graceful.

After dark, when the mother bird is on the nest, the least noise disturbs her. She will then snap her bill viciously in sharp contrast to her daytime gentleness, and all nearby birds will flutter and complain warningly in her behalf.

# Western Mockingbird

(MIMUS POLYGLOTTOS LEUCOPTERUS)

*Average length 10½ inches*

SURELY everyone knows and loves the *Mockingbird—all grayish drab with white showing abundantly on his black tail and wings as he flies.* He belongs to everyone, the rich and poor alike; lives anywhere, builds high or low—in alleys, along public right of ways, and in the finest landscaped gardens. Of all the birds that live he seems to suffer least from predatory cats. In town neighborhoods where cats abound he is able somehow to outwit them and manage, year after year, to hold his own.

He is the great commoner, giving freely to all—sometimes a bit lavishly when he sings for hours just outside your bedroom window, like one did to me last night. For a while I tried to think up some plan to discourage him, then my habit-ridden consciousness began to get his message. If sleep gets off man's arbitrary schedule, why call it the 'curse' of insomnia? Why not use the extra time of being fully alive as a gift—and enjoy it? Pick a happy thought and let the mind sing of it in the dark.

The *Mockingbird* himself is what we dismally call a 'poor sleeper', no doubt. He works hard at his job of singing all day, scarcely taking time to hunt food, you'd think he'd be worn out at night, yet, especially when the moon shines, the best he can do is to get a few cat naps—sounds like a hard life, doesn't it? He thinks differently. He knows that in the course of time he'll get all the sleep he actually needs—we all do, nobody dies of insomnia, no matter how they toss and rage. So, without arguing with Nature, he accepts this extra time and uses it gratefully to do a little practicing. Last night in a half-whisper, he was trying out some difficult imitations —how it sounds to start a cold motor, how to drive a nail in an empty room, and the unhappy complaint of the alley cat looking for trouble. In the full enjoyment of his work he mixed in ripples, trills, rolls, and dozens of the purest flights of imagination; but he started that engine, drove nail after nail, and put all the cats to shame. It was a priceless serenade but I went to sleep and missed the last part. The trouble is you can't stay awake after you really begin to enjoy insomnia.

*An opuntia cactus*

# *Phainopepla*

PHAINOPEPLA NITENS
*Average Length 7½ Inches*

**P**OETRY of motion in a realm of thorns — that is the *Phainopepla*. Look for him especially where the mistletoe hangs heavy in the mesquite, listen for him when his faint, whispered love song floats wraith-like in the soft desert dusk.

He is an aristocrat of such distinction he has no common name. The generic Greek word phainopepla means 'shining robe'; nothing less could serve this proud *jet black creature with wild, restless eyes of flaming scarlet, whose head bears a noble crest.* Flying upward he reveals *startling white patches on the under-wing feathers* which add a remarkable surprise element to his glossy perfection. He is co-extensive with the mesquite of the lower Sonoran life-zone and can be found nowhere else on earth. Don't miss him. Swarth says he is "totally different from any other North American bird".

Almost invariably he builds his home on a horizontal mesquite branch beneath a clump of mistletoe, well screened by its fringe of pendant stems. He uses only fine materials held together with spider web or stray hairs found caught on thorns where animals passed too near; and lines his small masterpiece with downy fluff pecked from desert seed pods of a year before.

The male is not only helpful but often does the major

part of this work, either under the eye of his *mouse gray, black-crested* loved one, or while she visits around the neighborhood. Later he takes his turn brooding the eggs, and there are records showing that if he loses his mate through mishap he assumes full responsibility, heroically feeding the nestlings all alone until they are able to fend for themselves.

There is no bird whose loveliness grips my heart like the *Phainopepla*.

# Cedar Waxwing

### BOMBYCILLA CEDRORUM
#### Average Length 7¼ Inches

A T first glance this high crested, exquisitely tinted *Waxwing* gives the general impression of merely a *fawn-colored* bird, but further inspection brings out many other colors. *His chin is definitely brown, upper tail coverts gray, underside white*, and other underparts *yellow shading to olive. His wings graduating from gray to black, edged with yellow, are further adorned, except for wing secondaries; with brilliant red tear-drops of wax-like substance. When the wings are folded they form a striking red spot, but the black, yellow-tipped tail feathers, never folded, reveal the showy line of waxy red balls, separate and perfect, at all times.*

It is thrilling to discover a flock of these beauties chattering and feeding in the spring sunshine, but seasons may pass without such opportunity. *Waxwings* never breed in the desert areas and their migratory habits are so erratic they come in numbers only when dried berries are plentiful. However, they are worth watching for and have always appeared before I have become completely discouraged.

# *Goldfinch*

(Spinus tristis pallidus)
*Average length 4½ inches*

SEVERAL books on birds have informed me that these exciting little black-browed balls of canary yellow would not be seen in my part of Arizona, but I know positively that I've had the luck to see them, to get so close I could almost touch them, and to stand there, holding my breath, under the spell of their glorious music. It seems incredible that such tiny bodies could produce such an enchanting volume of full, rich, rolling notes—very like but lacking the shrillness of the caged canary's best efforts.

These so-called *Pale Goldfinches* seem smaller to me than the standard sparrow though authorities give their size as the same, and certainly they are not 'pale'—they are the *most vivid yellow birds* I ever saw and the *black on brow and wings stands against the yellow* in unforgettable contrast. The bill is *corn yellow* but their *eyes are as black and glistening as wet coal*.

These *Goldfinches* come only on visits and it may be I have been exceptionally lucky to be around when they arrived. For this I am truly thankful, although it has put me in disagreement with several who have produced more impressive volumes.

# *House Finch*

(Carpodacus mexicanus)

*Average length 6 inches*

HOUSE FINCHES appear in greater abundance than any other single species in the southwestern areas. The careless sometimes call them *English Sparrows,* but anyone who could do that, is as far from being a judge of birds, as the *House Finch* is from being any kind of *Sparrow.* It is true they are little and busy like *Sparrows* and of more or less the same shape, but their markings are distinctly different.

The *House Finch* has a *deep rose, orange-red or, sometimes, scarlet forehead and eyeline* with a heavy patch of the *same shade on the back at the base of the tail.* Individuals vary as to tint of red. *Although his upperparts are brownish-gray* he is never streaked like the *Sparrow, and his throat and breast, and sometimes his whole head, are red*—certainly a clue to help anyone who takes a second glance.

*Finches* live in the desert country all the year round, nesting in early spring. Then it is they put on a major show—the straw dance—worthy of an Oscar in bird dramatics. First, the lover picks up a straw and struts to announce his honorable intentions. When he catches his lady's eye he performs every gyration in his power, in fact, he literally exhausts himself and often ends by falling limp at her feet, lying there like dead until she gives him a peck of interest on his breast— which instantly brings him to life. This does not end the courtship, however, since the lady is now ready to play 'hard--to-catch' and the ensuing chase turns into an endurance test.

The nest is finally built in cactus or brush, in cavity or nook of buildings or trees — they are not particular. It is shallow, cup-shaped, and constructed of rootlets, grass stems, heavy fibers, or whatever happens to be at hand, but it is always neat and compact. Then come three to six pale, greenish blue eggs, blotched around the large end with black or brown.

It is true the *House Finch* hobnobs with true *Sparrows* but, even in your mind, don't associate him with the *English Sparrow.* If you but once listen to his flow of song you will accord him his high place among the lavish givers.

(GAMBEL SPARROW)

# Sparrows

*Average length about 5 inches*

HAVING mentioned *Sparrows*, we'll try to clear the name—which, like Smith, is no distinction at all. For all who think 'sparrows is sparrows', I—a Smith—point to page 280, Volume 2, Book of Birds, published by the National Geographic Magazine. Here it is stated that "one hundred and nineteen kinds of sparrows are found on this continent north of Mexico. This list does not include the so-called 'English sparrow', (*Passer domesticus*), classified as one of the weaver finches of the Old World, which places it in a family different from the *Fringillidae* to which the North American sparrows belong".

The *Desert Black-throated Sparrow* has suffered most by comparison, (although side by side with the dowdy *chestnut-backed, white and black streaked English Sparrow* he is quite different). *Black covers his chin, throat and upper breast and comes to a point in the white of his underside. He shows strong white malar stripes against the deep brownish gray of his head, and his tail is truly black, with outside feathers white.* He is all over, especially in the more fertile areas, the year round, and in such numbers he cannot remain unnoticed.

During the winter months something much more special in *Sparrows*, dance sunlit cotillons on the lawns and along the desert edges. These *Sparrows* belong to the *White-crowned* group and are notable for their showy head trim, particularly the big *Gambel Sparrow*, the handsomest of them all. *His head stripes are clear-cut black and white and he is positively aristocratic.* He despises *English Sparrows* and drives them off his reservation before he joins in a chorus with the *Western Vesper*, the tiny *Brewer*, the *Western Lark* and others of the fifteen or more visiting varieties.

The constant musical undertone of all these gay fellows pervades the air but never dominates it except in the case of the *Black-throated* whose rapturous solo is one of the choicest pleasures offered by the desert. All are easily recognized by their sparrow-like figure although their striped head decorations show variety of tint and arrangement. The *Western Lark Sparrow* is the dressiest of them all, sporting even a fan-tail when making love.

# Cardinal

(RICHMONDENA CARDINALIS)

*Average length 9 inches*

CARDINALS are never really migratory, which trait results in there being several with state names, as the Florida, the Texas, and the Arizona *Cardinals,* all differing in some particular from each other and from those of Mexico and elsewhere. *His back is red as red need ever be but his head, with its proud high crest, his throat, and all below, flame with a more dazzling cardinal—a shade unmatched in the world of color. Around his heavy bill—grosbeak—he wears a circlet of black, broken only at the top.* It is in this single marking that *Cardinals* vary, some having the circlet unbroken, some having it heavier or thinner than others.

The *Cardinal* does not really like towns but thoroughly approves of the wide lawns and shade trees. When he flashes by other interests cease—when he pauses on a high limb and sends forth his brilliant, whistling call it is to every listener the perfect obligato to the prismatic desert air.

41

# Vermilion Flycatcher

(PYROCEPHALUS RUBINUS)

*Average length 5½ inches*

THE *Vermilion Flycatcher* breeds all over the Lower Sonoran life-zone and is so numerous it requires no great effort to know him. His Spanish name is all the introduction he needs—*brasita de fuego*, 'little coal of fire'.

*His globular, erectile crest and all his underparts, including wing linings, are the brightest possible scarlet; above he is grayish brown with black tail and black on upperside of wings.* It is startling to see this living flame flash overhead or to watch him guard his nest during that period of responsibility. He shoots into the air directly above it, hovers and floats there with grace and ease, all the while singing such a proud, twittering song he fills the world with joy.

The nest is a frail cup, always placed in trees, and the two or three eggs are buff, strikingly marked with brown and lavender. Like all *Flycatchers* he goes after all insects on the wing, with deadly aim and prodigious appetite.

# Verdin

(AURIPARUS FLAVICEPS)

*Average length 4½ inches*

THE incomparable *Verdin* is the smallest of our desert birds except the *Gnatcatcher* and, of course, the *Hummingbird*. And so shy it is almost necessary to find their nests first then wait patiently to see the little fellows themselves.

The nest will be in thorny mesquite, catsclaw, even cholla cactus, and on any short walk in the desert it is easy to discover a dozen—if you are that sort of person. To house so tiny a bird it is a bulky affair, about the size and shape of a large

Upper: *Vermilion Flycatcher*
Center: *Verdin*
Lower: *Black-tailed Gnatcatcher*

cocoanut, woven of thorn twigs, coarse grass, leaves and weed stems, thickly lined with feathers; the whole so firmly attached to the thorny branches on which it rests that it sways safely with the tree or bush even in the strongest wind.

If the thorns allow you to approach near enough you may find the wee mother peeping out of her round door, low in the side of the nest. She'll set up a surprising chatter and so will her mate hidden in the brush nearby. Both may even come into the open for they are peculiarly pugnacious when their privacy is invaded. Make them show themselves if you can—they are beautiful, with *heads of cloudy yellow and dainty bodies of tawny taupe with chestnut shoulder patches.*

When undisturbed their call notes are loud for their size, and resemble the happy chattering of the *Finches.* They are true desert dwellers, seemingly indifferent to heat and thirst, preferring areas incredibly remote from any known water supply. How their babies survive is another bird mystery I long to solve. All year on chilly nights the mother sleeps snugly in the brooding nest but her mate builds himself a separate roosting nest usually placed close by like any twin bed should be. His nest is never as elaborate and comfortable as hers—perhaps he's afraid of seeming to be a sissy.

# *Black-tailed Gnatcatcher*

(POLIOPTILA MELANURA)

*Average length 4½ inches*

THE slender *Black-tailed Gnatcatcher* belongs to the Old World family of Warblers. He is never conspicuous—*just all bluish gray, with a blackish crown and a long, narrow tail of solid black except for gray outer webs on the outside feathers.* But a bird with his colorful personality doesn't need bright feathers.

Like his kin in other parts of the world this westerner is intensely vivacious and tells all, in excited tones, like any neighborhood busybody. He gesticulates like a Frenchman, talks fast like a Mexican, and seems to make a good story out of nothing.

A frenzy of energy and vigor comes with nest building, brooding, and feeding the family, male and female working with equal bustle. Their nests turn out to be truly works of art—deeply cupped, exquisitely lined, and even decorated on the outside with any bits of color which can be forced to adhere. Now that's something! A bird that beautifies the premises to that extent is an asset to any neighborhood.

They are also fast workers in man's cause against the smaller insects and, since they are easy to entice, might well be sought after in cultivated gardens near the desert.

Hedgehog Cactus

# Killdeer

### (Charadrius vociferus)

#### *Average length 11 inches*

THE *Killdeer* is easily overlooked although he covers the desert waterfront — along the outermost main canals. This is because the coloration of this fresh water *Plover* all but blots him out, and his long speedy legs are always quick. Yet after he is once seen, he is actually a conspicuous bird and you wonder how you could have missed him before.

He is the size of a streamlined robin on stilts, and always impresses me as a *pure white-and-black bird, although he is reddish brown on the upper tail coverts. Between his globular black crown and long black bill he shows a high white forehead merging into white eye-patches. His long neck, all the way around, and his whole underside, including wing linings, are the purest white marked with two dead black neck bands, one a complete collar, the other lost near the black uppersides of his wings.* In flight, from the underside, he is a white bird with a black collar, but when he banks and turns he is a black bird with white markings.

This *Plover* belongs to one of the fastest flying families in the world and he stays in the air for hours at a time, giving his squeaky call—*kildee-kildee*—noticeable particularly at night. On the ground he holds his head high; and always stands high, like a sandpiper, on three toes, his foot lacking the back toe entirely. He runs amazingly fast with a springy, balancing gait.

The *Killdeer's* nest is merely a shallow saucer trampled in dry ground, generally near water but sometimes surprisingly far away. The three or four sharply pointed gray, olive green, and black mottled eggs are always placed points down to the middle of the nest. Although the nests are absolutely unconcealed they blend so perfectly with the ground they are peculiarly difficult to see. The babies arrive running, hardly wait to be dried before they start out to see the world.

I saw a *Killdeer* do his 'strut dance' once, just as daylight dimmed toward dusk. He was all alone, the world forgotten. In fact I edged up very near him and stood unnoticed for fully twenty minutes. All his motions, even his low, chuckling exultations were remarkably like those of a turkey gobbler except that his tail was not held erect but fanned straight backward or dipped downward with quivering ecstasy. He swayed from side to side, dragging first one wing then the other. His head kept time with his feet and he danced in every feather—bursting with the joy of being alive, not trying to impress anybody.

*That's true enthusiasm for life — dancing alone in the desert!*

# Hummingbirds

*Black-chinned* (Archilochus alexandri)
*Costa* (Calypte costae)
*Rufous* (Selasphorous rufus)

THERE are more than six hundred kinds of *Hummingbirds,* all natives of the western hemisphere, with headquarters near the equator in South America. Only sixteen are found regularly in North America, north of Mexico, all sixteen being known in Arizona in varying numbers. They range the entire west, only the *Ruby-throated* going east of the Mississippi river. Observers agree that the *Black-chinned* is most abundant in Arizona's famous Valley of the Sun.

*Upper Right: Rufous Hummingbird*
*Upper Left: Costa Hummingbird*
*Lower: Black-chinned Hummingbird*

Their iridescent wings are narrow and pointed with a spread of less than four inches yet these tiny birds achieve a mile a minute, and during migration travel fully six hundred miles. They can fly backward, straight up, or poise for long moments in the air—feats beyond other birds. The rapidity of their wing-beat does it. In "Bird Flight", by Gordon C. Aymar, the number of their strokes is given as two hundred per second, estimated by comparing the vibrations set in motion by a violin note with those of the bird's wing. He said the best the *Sparrow* could do was thirteen strokes per second—yet even he gets around.

All birds are more or less pneumatic, their organs floating on air sacs inside their springy bone structure, with the development of the keel bone controlling the wing power. In the *Hummingbird* this breast bone is extraordinarily deep and strong in proportion to the size of his wings and the burden they carry.

His heart beats are unbelievably rapid, also his breathing; and he has more red corpuscles in his few drops of blood than any other living thing. His body temperature runs up to 111 degrees—but he doesn't perspire (no birds do). Whole books are written about *Hummingbirds* but nothing can explain to me the miracle of their existence—their speed, endurance, and magic beauty.

The *Black-chinned Hummingbird has a bronze-green back, white collar, and metallic violet markings; the Costa also, is bronze-green with head, gorget, and flaring ruff a glittering amethyst,* so iridescent it seems, under varying lights, to run through all the tints of the rainbow; *the Rufous is bright reddish brown with elongated gorget of sparkling scarlet.*

A test tube of sweetened water hung on a twig with a red ribbon will bring *Hummingbirds* into any garden so that they may be seen quite clearly. They might even build nests close by, and that is something rare to watch.

The dainty three and a half inch mother needs a cup only the size of half an egg shell for her nest. This she fashions of spider web and plant down in the crotch of swaying twigs, sometimes near the ground, sometimes high above. She lays two white eggs like gleaming pearls, and these she will protect with her life as she waits for her frightfully ugly, insect-like babies to be hatched. They arrive naked and blind with stubby, flat bills — only a mother could stand the shock—yet in fourteen to twenty days they leave the nest, strong-winged, long-billed jewels able to find their own living in the hearts of deepest flowers, or to flash through the air over land and sea, even to the faraway Andes in equatorial South America.

Two things always puzzled me most when a child; one was, how any bird stayed on a perch during sleep, and the other, what happened after the *Hummingbird's* bill entered the blossom—other birds drink by raising their heads. I don't know which mystery was solved first, but I was relieved to find that birds sleep safely because of an automatic muscle which tightens the tendon running along the leg bone when they sit down. This contracts the toes around the perch so securely they must be wide enough awake to consciously raise the body in order to let loose at all.

The *Hummingbird* puzzle is explained by his extensile tongue, twice the length of his bill when unfolded. With this he laps deep into the flower, collects the nectar, and doubles it back into his throat. Mother Nature always finds a way.

Experiments are now going on to record the *Hummingbird's* song. His notes are so high pitched the human ear can catch only a faintest ghost of the sound, but radio and recording experts may prove he has a complicated and exquisite repertoire.

# Blackbirds

(Agelaius phoeniceus)

*Average length 9 inches*

(Xanthocephalus xanthocephalus)

*Average length 10½ inches*

BOTH *Redwing* and *Yellow-headed Blackbirds* have always clouded the sky in the lower parts of Arizona, but since irrigation has so greatly extended cultivation they are here in ever increasing numbers, raucous swarms of them in the cottonwoods, the alfalfa, the grain fields, and clutters of them on the highways where the *Redwings* flash their stoplights impudently in front of your car.

They are big and *black* but never somber. The larger *Yellowheads* need no further description beyond their name except that *the deep orange yellow of their heads extends low on the breast and there is a patch of white on each wing. The Redwing is all black except for gorgeous scarlet epaulettes on his shoulders* which he fluffs to show he is happy. When he is feeling low and small he parks himself in utter blackness with his lights switched off.

Both of these showy *Blackbirds* build swinging-basket nests between reeds in wet localities and breed several times each year striving for some semblance of separate homelife through noisy, undignified brawls. No disturbance of the air, no static during the worst of storms, is more distressing to the human ear than a few hundred *Blackbirds* arbitrating personal arguments. They choke and screech like their machinery needed oil—and sound shockingly profane.

# *Hooded Oriole*

### (ICTERUS CUCULLATUS)

*Average length 7 inches*

THE *Orioles* of the desert wear more yellow per bird than *Orioles* living elsewhere. Of the three, *Bullock's, Scott's* and the *Hooded,* the latter wears the most of all. Designers should start a fad for *Oriole yellow;* it has a quality all its own—it is a color in itself and when emphasized by the desert sunshine it makes the *Hooded Oriole* beyond description or comparison. With his *black wings and tail and his masklike black throat-patch against his yellow body* he is positively gaudy.

Except for short mid-winter visits into Mexico this brilliant ornament adorns the desert his whole life through. By April, sometimes towards the end of March, he is back home in large numbers.

They breed from early spring well into the summer, fashioning cup-shaped, semi-pensile nests in eucalyptus or other trees, but most often on the under sides of palm fronds. Here they tie or sort of sew their shallow baskets of palm fibers to the leaf with long threads stripped from the leaf itself; an incredible feat, it would seem, with only bill and claw for tools.

The love life of *Orioles* is notably individualistic. Some observers assert the male builds in bachelorhood and wins his wife on the merits of his work — leaving all further home economics to her. Others state the female builds alone or with his help; also, that females often fight over finished nests until they are wrecked beyond use.

In his book, "Birds of California", Dawson tells of a pair building four times one July, either trial or decoy nests—or perhaps the male was changing mates and starting a new nest with each romance. Life in a social set like that could never be dull.

The tones of the *Oriole's* call notes and short songs are rich, never loud, and most difficult to imitate or suggest. They are never heard in down-town traffic but add much to the joy of life in gardens and on ranches round-about.

All *Orioles* are active, independent citizens and very valuable in keeping down the devastating caterpillar hordes by eating the larvae.

# Western Kingbird

(Tyrannus verticalis)

*Average length 9 inches*

THE *Western Kingbird,* always numerous, is increasing
with the vegetation in the lower valleys. He appears to
be simply a *grayish bird with a black tail, narrowly edged
with white,* although *his underparts are yellowish and on top
of his head he wears a bright red spot, revealed only at times.*

Although a true king among birds he is not the all-out
tyrant variety as he shows no inclination to interfere with
neighbors in good standing. However, with all others he is
utterly fearless and brooks no foolishness from marauders
whatever their size may be. In desert country where trees are
at a premium *Kingbirds* build their nests in all sorts of extra-
ordinary locations, high or low, always sure of being able to
police their premises. *Kingbirds* are so particularly watchful
and belligerent in regard to *Hawks,* all ranchers who do not

keep bees, will readily welcome them around their chicken yards. With bee keepers it is entirely a different matter.

The *Kingbird* has a sweet tooth and enjoys honey bees in place of candy. When the craving takes hold of him he is said to flash that red spot on top of his head. The bees mistake it for an innocent flower and the *Kingbird* gets a treat.

# Horned Lark

(OTOCORIS ALPESTRIS)

*Average length 7¾ inches*

UNLESS you have the bird lover's second sight you may miss this regular desert winter visitor. The *Horned Lark* lives always on the ground which is so like the *pale coloration* of his own coat, he must move to be seen at all. If you do catch sight of him *his black horn-like tufts* show clearly against the *pinkish cinnamon of his head*.

These elusive birds seem entirely independent of water but no doubt, however deep they may go into the desert, they must know of some hidden supply, for their food, being dried seeds, does not furnish even the moisture to be had from insects.

They give their characteristic lark music mostly from the ground but, at any hour of the day, they may fly high in the air, float gracefully, and sing with true lark abandon. Like too many winter visitors, these mountain loving birds rush away before the lavish desert spring brings to the palo verdes their season of golden glory.

# *Abert's Towhee*

### (PIPILO ABERTI)

### *Average length 9 inches*

ABERT'S TOWHEE is not a dressy bird but he has a friendly personality and is ready to be fed almost from your hand, certainly from any hospitable windowsill. He makes social calls to the fertile areas and well into the foot-hills practically all winter, breeds here in summer, and is seen well into October. If he leaves at all during the year it is late in the fall and his stay away is not long.

If small flocks of *grayish brown birds, with pinkish brown underparts shading to buff,* come begging in your dooryard they'll be these sprightly *Towhees,* well worth your friendly attention. They have a high-pitched, snappy little chatter among themselves but no distinctive song. They are so well-mannered they are usually considered timid birds but they are never so shy that a sprinkle of walnut meats will fail to break down all reserve.

Of all the *Towhees, Abert's* is the largest. They love the mesquite and nest in its protection, building large, bulky, dish-like affairs of almost any coarse material.

# Cooper's (Summer) Tanager

## (Piranga rubra cooperi)

*Average length 7 inches*

IN names and markings the *Southwestern Tanagers* are confusing. The *Western Tanager* and the *Arizona Hepatic Tanager* breed only in the mountains while *Cooper's Tanager* breeds throughout the lower Sonoran life-zone; all very shy birds and hard to find.

*Upper: Abert's Towhee*
*Lower: Cooper's Tanager*

Florence Merriam Bailey gives this warning in her "Birds of New Mexico", "The young field student may well be on his guard when among *Cooper's Tanagers*, for the immature male, after molting the female yellowish dress, may acquire only a few red body feathers, or a wholly red dress. Between these extremes, as Dr. Chapman points out, 'there is every degree of intergradation'." Pictures in color invariably show *Cooper's Tanagers as clear vermilion red in every feather* so it is undoubtedly this unreliability, coupled with their isolationistic tendencies, that keeps them on the 'rarely seen' list of most observers. Casual observers 'see' them frequently but it is probable that the *Vermilion Flycatcher* is often confused with the elusive *Cooper's Tanager.*

# Dwarf Cowbird
### (Molothrus ater obscurus)
*Average length 7½ inches*

D WARF COWBIRDS are without manners or morals —and not even pretty to look at; but they are here in such numbers I must point at least an accusing finger at them. *The male is black with a brown head, the female all dullish brown; no contrasting markings on either sex.*

In the cultivated sections or far out in the desert they are always in numerous proportion to the number of birds about them. They aren't particular where they live so long as they can find plenty of ready built nests into which they can smuggle their eggs to be cared for by their hapless hosts. The nice little *Gnatcatcher* seems to be the *Cowbird's* favorite victim. Sometimes her meticulous little nest is hardly completed before the watching poacher slips in and deposits her own large egg, giving it a headstart over the owner's eggs which come later. The baby *Cowbird* is a vociferous beggar and, being hatched first, is strong enough to beg the mother bird out of most of the food she brings to the nest. It is

DWARF COWBIRD

pathetic to see a tiny *Gnatcatcher* working her feathers to the bone trying to satisfy the alien gourmand who grows, in about ten days, to be as large as she is. Her own babies are starved, trampled, or pushed out of the nest, but the *Cowbird* lingers on, then later, follows her around begging so hard he is often fed for days after he is plenty able to provide for himself.

Besides the tricks and traits of *Cowbird* babyhood these unlovely waifs of the desert go on for months waylaying any birds they see, still begging for food. They have no pride at all, and no conscience; and their high, insistent demand for food is their only vocal achievement.

No, the *Cowbird* is not nice at all, but if you didn't know him before, you are now in position to recognize him, and dislike him personally—as I do.

# White-rumped Shrike

(LANIUS LUDOVICIANUS EXCUBITORIDES)

*Average length 10 inches*

IT surprises me that the stubby *White-rumped Shrike* is so often mistaken for the streamlined *Mockingbird*. He not only differs in shape but in his thick, hooked bill, his bridled eyes, and his big predacious feet. Also, his upper parts are *a lighter slate gray, darker on the head; tail and wings black, edged with white; and his whole underside is white only faintly barred with gray.*

He earns the nickname 'butcher bird' by impaling his small prey on thorns or barbed wire while he goes blithely hunting more for the love of killing. Since he sometimes kills smaller birds he is the most despised outcast in all of birdland, but only the *Mockingbird* is big enough and public spirited enough to scold him to his face. The *Shrike* takes all insults stoically, moves on slowly with a more or less resigned manner, and forever sits alone.

You can easily see him—on a cactus or a fence post, watching for any small, moving thing. At intervals he sails down slowly, not beginning to fly until he is fairly low, then he crowds his prey—rodent, sand squirrel, lizard, small bird —until he can light on it with his heavy feet. He does not tear it with his talons but holds it down and cripples it with his wicked bill or carries it immediately to a thorn and hangs it there to dry and finally die. Sometimes he goes back later to eat his 'jerky', but not always if hunting is good.

The fact that *Shrikes* eat pecks of crickets, grasshoppers and other baleful insects has protected him from being declared by man an enemy bird; he is not even listed as harmful. But the birds don't like him and I can't entirely approve of his methods.

# Swainson Hawk

(BUTEO SWAINSONI)

*Average length 19½ inches*

WHEN a *Hawk* is in sight he is sure to be noticed, particularly in a desert landscape. He is so robust, so powerful and so menacing I can't imagine loving one, but he is fascinating and, if understood in all his activities, is appreciated by all desert people for his service in controlling the snake and rodent population.

The *Swainson Hawk*, perhaps the most valuable hawk in the world, is truly a friend of the western rancher. His unrelenting campaign against gophers, rabbits, and grasshoppers gives many a poor rancher his only chance to work his irrigated acres at all.

Although his *upperparts are a uniform dark brown, he is easily identified, because he wears a sharply contrasting reddish brown chest band on his striking white vest.*

This *Hawk* is a strong, high flier and works his territory with great diligence, but he is also frequently seen standing guard on a high saguaro, perhaps above his bulky nest in a crotch of one of the saguaro limbs. At least he claims it is a nest. It looks more like a half-bale of hay lodged between trunk and limb, and held precariously by the spines of the cactus. But the *Swainsons* live in it, raise their babies, and are a part of the populous saguaro community. They are scolded and frowned upon by the smaller tenants of the more luxurious suites, but never turn on them nor molest them unless hunting is so poor they must catch smaller birds to keep their own babies alive.

Eagles, vultures, condors, all belong to the *Hawk* family, in fact, there are about seven hundred forms on the major list. All are important, not only in the bird world but in man-made economies. In America the Eagle is elevated to glamorous heights, and the vulture is a respected garbage collector, but otherwise the hand and gun of man is against the tribe in general. Agriculturists declare this a foolish policy, which is common sense, of course—but still fails to make it possible to love a *Hawk*. They always fascinate me but I never watch one without a shudder.


# Western Red-tailed Hawk

(BUTEO BOREALIS CALURUS)

*Average length 20 inches*

THE *Western Red-tailed Hawk* is oftenest seen on a cushion of thorns at the tip of the highest saguaro, gazing intently over the sun-drenched desert floor. Or, soaring in the graceful, wide circles of a slow flier, when his *prominent red tail markings* become visible.

His upper parts are a *dark, sooty brown, marked with lighter brown and white,* and *his tail,* his distinguishing feature, *is a bright reddish brown.* From below, *his light breast* and *darkish streaks* are clearly to be seen.

He swoops accurately upon his prey with a high-pitched scream, stirring in its wild savagery. He enjoys gophers, sand squirrels, kangaroo rats (and all other varieties); is very fond of rabbits, snakes, lizards, and does not disdain a skunk upon occasion. Besides his main meals he eats grasshoppers like we do salted peanuts—whenever and as long as they are in reach.

Year after year the same ones return to their favorite lookout towers. They seem to love certain spots.

As *Hawks* go, the *Western Red-tailed* is a noble fellow, and so much a part of Saguaroland you will certainly see him sooner or later.

*WESTERN RED-TAILED HAWK*

# Burrowing Owl

(SPEOTYTO CUNICULARIA)

*Average length 10 inches*

THE *Burrowing Owl* is given to you last—but not because he is least among my bird friends. Quite the op-
posite, he is one of my first and best; and, of all, would be
the hardest to forget.

During my first days of living alone in the desert the
*Meadowlark* did much to steady my morale, while this
friendly little *Owl*, before he became a solace, filled at least
my first night with panic. The sky was wide and remote, the
horizon abnormally far away, and the silence complete and
unrelenting—I went to bed that first night feeling suspended
in mysterious space. Very soon dozens of little *Owls* came out
of their holes in the ground, sat before their doorways, and
fell to gossiping about the doings of the day. They seemed
to closely encircle my sleeping porch in multitudes and to
spread out over the whole wide desert.

*Burrowing Owls* sound like no other *Owls* on earth;
they make no semblance of the recognizable hoot-hoot;
their's is an eerie, aspirated inquiry sung out with monoto-
nous, ghostlike intensity, always with an ascending inflection.
They literally leave you up in the air. That night as they
called back and forth in the darkness my imagination stag-
gered under a load of its own fashioning. I had no idea what
I'd find inhabiting my immediate vicinity—if I escaped until
morning. But even at earliest dawn I could not see a living
thing as far as the eye could reach, and it was a nervous long
while before the milk boy told me "them's just little billy
owls, you'd ought to see how funny they look".

And I did one day—*standing tall on his long, bare legs,
a round-faced, short-tailed, dull brown little fellow with*

*white spots and bars all over.* As *Owls* go he didn't look so very funny, I thought, but the trick he did there on the canal bank of 'twisting his head off' was comical enough to entertain me immensely, as well as a little Mexican boy who happened to be passing. As the boy approached, the *Owl* looked him squarely in the eye, nodding 'how-do-you-do' at each step forward. At about ten feet the boy began to circle, slowly at first, and the *Owl's* eyes followed him round. Faster and faster the boy circled, faster and faster the little *Owl's* head went round. Never could a human eye be quick enough to detect any fake about the performance; the *Owl's* head simply went round and round; his eyes never left the boy's eyes, they followed him in full, complete circles. That is exactly what my eyes saw! In spite of myself I expected to see that little head twisted off, and come rolling toward me in the dust. But, the boy gave up first, and with unruffled dignity the *Owl* made a final bow and backed off the stage.

Of course the unscrupulous fakir had turned his head just so far and then, with lightning quickness, flipped it back and started round again, but it takes an artist to get away with a trick like that, and I hold the 'billy owl' to be the world's top-liner.

There is some desert gossip about *Burrowing Owls* living in the same holes with badgers and rattlesnakes, but those who should know say this is on the scandal side—that there is no triangle there at all. The truth is the *Owls* set up house-keeping in abandoned holes of any kind to save themselves from learning the art of digging their own.

They forage in good weather, principally but not always at night, and store abundant supplies all along their runways. Sometimes a dozen will live in one hole and help each other keep watch at the flimsy barricade of trash they build around the entrance. When disturbed they bounce up and down like popcorn before dashing underground. They eat beetles, grasshoppers, cactus fruits, and weed seeds, and seem to enjoy life more than do most *Owls* who take life more seriously.

If I ever live alone in the desert again I want lots of 'billy owls' to live around me and to call in the night—just to assure me that the overpowering silence out there can be dealt with in a normal way.

## Editor's Note:

*When Gusse Thomas Smith first wrote her "birds of the Southwestern Desert" most, if not all, of "her birds" were encountered in and around the nearby desert areas.*

*Now, as the desert gives way to development and more and more of the desert itself is stripped and overrun, the once populous birds have retreated to distant and isolated surroundings.*

*Several of the more adventuresome species remain and are to be seen now and then. Most however, especially the confirmed desert dwellers, are rarely to be found and then only in remote locations.*

*Our vanishing desert bird-life is another of the hidden costs of "progress". It points up the growing need for established sanctuaries, especially for bird-life indigenous to unusual terrain such as deserts or marsh lands.*

*The Audubon Society and other wildlife groups are working continuously to save our disappearing birds. These organizations deserve the help and involvement of all of us.*

*Through them nature-lovers have a voice and the means to do something about the threat of extinction facing so many species . . . . before it is too late.*